The Ultimate Billie Eilish Fan Book 2023/4

100+ Billie Eilish Facts, Quiz, Photos & More

JAMIE ANDERSON

BELLANOVA

MELBOURNE · SOFIA · BERLIN

Contents

Billie Eilish
INTRODUCTION

Since uploading her single *Ocean Eyes* to
Soundcloud in 2015, Billie has taken the
world by storm. Famous for her out-there
fashion style, chilled-out attitude and husky
vocals, Billie is one superstar that is here to
stay.

So how much do you really know about
Billie? In this book you will learn how she
became famous, what her childhood was like
and much more. Then, test yourself in the
quiz at the end! Are you ready? *Let's go!*

Billie Eilish

FAMILY & CHILDHOOD

Billie was born on December 18, 2001 in Los Angeles, California. She was conceived through IVF treatment.

She grew up in the suburb of Highland Park in Los Angeles. Billie said there was a lot of crime in her neighborhood and her neighbors got arrested by the FBI for money laundering!

Billie's full name is Billie Eilish Pirate Baird O'Connell.

Billie's starsign is Sagitarrius.

Her parents are Maggie Baird and Patrick O'Connell.

Her mother, Maggie, is an actress who has performed on Broadway as well as on television shows such as *Bones, The X-Files* and *Six Feet Under*. She even released an album in 2009 called *We Sail*.

" *Pretty much my whole life, I've been a performer and have loved singing and writing songs in my room for my own ears.* "

–Billie Eilish

Billie's father is also an actor and musician. He has been on several TV shows and movies, and plays the piano and ukulele. He is of Irish/Scottish descent.

Billie's parents both travel and work with her on her tours.

Billie has one brother called Finneas, who is four years older than her. You've probably heard of him though, he's *almost* as famous as Billie herself!

Billie and Finneas are very close friends, and he co-wrote all the songs on her debut album. You can also see him perform with her when they are on tour.

When Billie was younger she was scared of singing in front of people. She would stuff her face into a pillow and then sing.

Finneas is also a great actor. He played the role of Alistair in the TV series *Glee*, and had a part in *Modern Family*.

"

I'm gonna make what I want to make, and other people are gonna like what they're gonna like. It doesn't really matter."

– Billie Eilish

Finneas and Billie were both homeschooled by their parents. Their parents wanted them to pursue whatever they were interested in, and they spent a lot of time learning about music and songwriting.

When Billie was eight years old she joined the *Los Angeles Children's Chorus*. She said that the choir really helped her to develop her voice and taught her how to sing properly.

Billie wrote her first song when she was 11 years old for her mom's songwriting class. The song was inspired by *The Walking Dead*, and is about the zombie apocalypse!

Billie went to a few acting auditions when she was younger, but didn't really enjoy it. She did provide background dialogue for crowd scenes in some pretty cool movies, though, including *Diary of a Wimpy Kid* and the *X-Men Series*.

Billie is 5 feet 3 inches (1.61 m) tall.

Billie took dance classes until she was 16. However, during one performance her hip muscle came apart from her bone, forcing her to quit dancing and focus more on music.

When Billie was six, she learnt to play *I Will* by the Beatles on the Ukulele.

As well as working closely with Billie, her brother Finneas has co-written and produced songs for Selena Gomez, Justin Bieber, Camila Cabello and others.

Billie's first name was in honor of her paternal grandfather. *Eilish* was inspired by a conjoined twin her parents saw in a documentary, and *Pirate* was Finneas' choice!

Billie Eilish
EARLY CAREER

Billie started writing songs with her brother Finneas in 2015, when she was 13. Finneas was already in a band and had been producing and writing songs for several years.

• • •

The first songs that Finneas and Billie recorded together were called *She's Broken* (written by Finneas) and *Fingers Crossed* (written by Billie). They put them up on Soundcloud.

The first song that Billie released on her own was *Ocean Eyes*. Her dance teacher asked her and Finneas to record a song to dance to. It was originally written for Finneas' band *The Slightlys*, but he decided it was better for Billie's voice. They then uploaded it to Soundcloud for her dance teacher to download.

• •

In just a couple of weeks, *Ocean Eyes* had hundreds of thousands of listens! This is when Finneas' manager, Danny Rukasin, asked him about Billie. He thought she had amazing potential.

It was in January 2016, that Billie was signed to a division of Apple Music, where they prepare up-and-coming artists for the big time. She had a stylist from Chanel and a publicist that helped shape her style into the Billie we know and love today.

• • •

Two months after signing to Apple Music, Billie released a music video for her song *Ocean Eyes* on her Youtube channel. It was very popular, and some of the biggest names in the music industry praised it.

• • •

Her next single, *Six Feet Under*, was released on June 23, 2016. The music video was homemade, and her mom did the editing!

"

I don't know how to function without music. When I'm not making it, I'm listening to it. It gives me courage and takes care of my mind."

– Billie Eilish

Later that year, in August, Billie was finally signed to a record label — *Darkroom and Interscope Records*. Her manager re-released her first two singles to streaming platforms such as Spotify.

• • •

The year of 2017 was very busy for Billie (and Finneas!). She released two EPs, and seven singles!

• •

Billie's first festival performance was at *South by Southwest* in March 2017. She also did her first tour, the *Don't Smile at Me* tour, in October that year.

Billie's manager arranged a deal with Spotify to promote her music, which made a huge impact on her early success. Of course, now everyone knows who she is!

• • •

Billie's first EP release was '*don't smile at me*'. It was released on August 11, 2017.

• • •

In 2019, shortly after her debut album was released, Billie became the youngest person to have 1 billion streams on Spotify!

Billie Eilish
HITTING THE
BIG TIME

Billie's singing voice is soprano. Her voice is often described as 'ethereal'.

• • •

Billie released her first full album on March 19th, 2019. It included the hit singles *'bad guy'*, *'when the party's over'*, *'you should see me in a crown'* and *'bury a friend'*.

Billie's debut album, *When We Fall Asleep, Where Do We Go?*, made her the first artist born in the 2000's to top the albums chart!

• • •

In 2020, Billie became the second, and youngest, artist to win the top four awards at the **Grammys**: *Best New Artist, Song of the Year, Record of the Year,* and *Album of the Year.* She also won a fifth award for *Best Pop Vocal Album*!

• • •

In February 2021, Billie released her first documentary on Apple TV+: *Billie Eilish: The World's a Little Blurry*. It gives you a great behind-the-scenes view of her rise to fame.

Billie is the youngest female artist to have a number one album in the UK.

• • •

Billie recorded two songs for the popular TV series *13 Reasons Why*: *'bored'* and *'lovely'*, which she recorded with Khalid.

• • •

In March 2023, Billie Eilish rocked her acting debut in Amazon Prime Video's *Swarm*. She played Eva, the leader of a cult inspired by NXIVM, and got rave reviews for her performance.

"There are alway going to be bad things. But you can write it down and make a song out of it."

– Billie Eilish

During the COVID-19 pandemic, in July 2020, Billie released the single *My Future*. She told Apple Music, *"the future feels uncertain and crazy right now but I think we need to be ready to put the work in, and if we do that, we should be hopeful and excited for our future."*

• • •

Billie's long-awaited second studio album was released on July 30, 2021.

It is called *Happier Than Ever*, and includes the singles 'My Future', 'Therefore I Am' and 'Your Power', as well as 13 other tracks that she co-wrote with her brother.

In March 2021, Billie released her first book. It is a biography through pictures from her childhood until now. She also released an audiobook version.

• • •

Billie and Finneas wrote and recorded the theme song for the latest James Bond movie. The song is called *No Time to Die* and it hit the top of the charts around the world when it was released. It was her first #1 single in the UK.

• • •

Billie and Finneas won the Oscar for *Best Original Song* in 2022, making Billie the first person born in the 21st century to win an Academy Award!

" In real life, I'm a really smiley person. I smile when I talk and I laugh. "

– Billie Eilish

Billie was the opening act for Florence and the Machine on her 2018-2019 tour.

• • •

Billie has done six headlining tours and her 2022 *Happier Than Ever: The World Tour*, started in New Orleans, USA on February 3rd and ended on Guadalajara, Mexico on April 2nd 2023. She played 88 shows in total!

• • •

In Billie's song '*NDA*', she talks about struggling with fame — in particular relationships. NDA is short for Non-Disclosure Agreement.

Over her career so far, Billie has been nominated for 366 major awards and won 172. Some of her wins include seven Grammy Awards, three Billboard Music Awards, three BRIT Awards and an Academy Award! Impressive.

• • •

Billie has broken two *Guinness World Records*. She held the record for '*Most simultaneous US Hot 100 entries by a female*' until Taylor Swift took over in 2019. Billie still holds the record for '*youngest female at No. 1 on the UK albums chart*'.

One of Billie's most successful singles was *Bad Guy*, which she also recorded with her idol, Justin Bieber.

• • •

Billie also featured in Justin Bieber's Youtube Originals series, *Justin Bieber: Seasons*. You can see her in episode 10.

• • •

Billie and Finneas wrote three songs for the Pixar movie, *Turning Red*.

• • •

On July 21st 2022, Billie surprised fans by releasing a two-track EP called *Guitar Songs*. She wanted to release it early as she believed the message was very current and important.

In 2022, Billie became the youngest ever performer to headline Glastonbury Festival in the UK! She also performed at Coachella Music Festival that summer.

• • •

Billie was a guest on the final episode of The Ellen Degeneres Show in May 2022. She told Ellen that she has already started thinking about her third studio album, and hopes to create it in 2023. We are still waiting in hope!

• • •

In 2023, Billie wrote the song *"What Was I Made For"* for the movie Barbie. It became her second number one single in the UK.

Billie Eilish

Billie likes to keep her relationships private. She says the times that she has told the world about them, she has regretted it.

• •

The one relationship she was open about was with rapper Brandon 'Q' Adams. They broke up in 2019, and she talks about their relationship on her documentary.

Billie was dating actor Matthew Tyler Vorce, but it is believed they broke up in early 2022.

Billie has Tourrettes Syndrome. This means that she sometimes gets involuntary tics and movements. She has said that every day is different and she is learning to deal with it.

Billie is known for her baggy clothing and crazy fashion. She says she knows she dresses pretty weird.

Billie chooses to wear baggy clothes so that she is not sexualized and people don't judge her.

Billie has always been a huge Belieber. Now, her and Justin Bieber are very close friends! Justin has said he is very protective over her.

Billie first met Justin Bieber at Coachella, and his manager Scooter Braun posted an adorable video of the moment they met on Instagram.

Deadly fever, please don't ever break; Be my reliever 'cause I don't self medicate."

— My Strange Addiction

Billie is a huge animal lover, and was raised vegetarian. She has been **vegan** since 2014.

In 2019, PETA gave her the *'Best Voice for Animals'* award, for her advocacy against the dairy, wool and meat industries.

Billie dated actor Jesse Rutherford from October 2022 to May 2023. She posted on Instagram in October 2023 that she "couldn't be more single."

Billie openly supported Joe Biden during the 2021 presidential elections and performed at the 2020 Democratic National Convention.

She has at least two tattoos. One of which she said, *"I did get a tattoo but you won't ever see it."*

Billie has two dogs and one cat. Her dog Pepper has been in the family for many years and she adopted a Pit Bull puppy in 2020. Her cat Misha is a rescue cat.

At the beginning of her career, Billie used to read all of her social media comments and DMs, but stopped doing it as people were so negative.

In April 2019, Billie released a clothing collaboration with Takashi Murakami called *Blōhsh*. She has recently expanded into kids clothing, too.

Billie still lives at home, in the same house she grew up in, although her song lyrics suggest she also secretly bought a house when she was 17! It used to belong to singer Leona Lewis. Her brother moved out in 2019, but still lives closeby.

Billie is passionate about environmental issues and filmed a video in 2019 with actor Woody Harrelson about the dangers of climate change.

Billie Eilish

Billie hates smiling—in public at least. She says it makes her feel weak and powerless. However, she smiles a lot in private!

• • •

Billie runs her own social media. She wants to engage honestly and naturally with her fans.

Her favorite TV show is *The Office*. She has even used lines from the show in her song *My Strange Addiction*!

• •

Billie has never used drugs or smoked.

• •

Billie had her teeth straightened. She used Invisalign.

• •

During a dentist appointment, Billie recorded the sound of the whirring drill to use in her song *Bury a Friend*.

Nails are important to Billie! She loves having long, pointy, bright-colored nails. However, she once accidentally ripped a nail off—the photo is online, but it's not for the faint-hearted!

• • •

Billie may be famous for her crazy hair colors, but she is actually a natural blonde!

• • •

Her favorite movie is *Fruitvale Station* starring Michael B. Jordan.

" *People are terrified of me, and I want them to be.* "

– Billie Eilish

Billie is lactose intolerant.

• • ·

Billie is very active on social media, and it's a great way to get to know her better. Her handles are **@billieeilish** on Instagram and Twitter and **billie-eilish** on Snapchat.

• •

When Billie revealed her blonde hair in an Instagram post in March 2021 (after fans thought she was wearing a wig at the 2021 Grammys), it became the fastest Instagam photo to reach 1 million likes in history. It took six minutes!

Some of Billie's early music influences were *The Beatles, Justin Bieber, Green Day, Linkin Park* and *Lana Del Rey*. Her favorite genre of music is hip-hop.

• •

Billie played herself in an episode of Sesame Street in 2022. You can watch her on the episode *Elmo's Number Adventure*.

• •

In June 2021, Billie was on the front cover of *British Vogue* magazine, wearing a corset. The photoshoot showed a very different side to Billie.

If I'm in a bad mood, or if I'm uncomfortable, it's probably what I'm wearing that's making me feel that way"

– Billie Eilish

Billie really likes fancy cars, and has said she'd like to design one one day.

• • •

Although she probably has many pairs of shoes, the ones she is most often photographed in are the limited edition Nike Air Force 1 High PSNY.

• • •

Billie calls her fans 'family'.

• • •

In November 2021, Billie released her vegan and cruelty-free perfume brand, "Eilish".

Billie Eilish QUOTES

Billie may be just 21, but she's got some serious wisdom in those song lyrics of hers.

Sure, she's a bit silly and can make us laugh, but guess what? She's also got some seriously inspiring quotes up her sleeve. Check out a few of our faves...

"Time is kind of an amazing thing because you can do so much with it. I think people underestimate time... I don't want to just sit on my phone for hours."

• • •

"[Justin Bieber] was like my first love. That was the person I was in love with, in my head he was in love with me, it was like a relationship with a person."

• • •

"I've always done whatever I want and always been exactly who I am."

"I go through a lot of depression, and I know other people do, too, but I have an outlet that so many people don't. If you have that inside of you and can't get it out, what do you do?"

• • •

"As young people we have to own and use our power to make a difference. When we go into the voting booth, it's about deciding who will lead America into the future."

• • •

"I don't think a song should be put in a category."

"Nothing really scares me, to be honest."

· • •

"I feel like I write so that people can think of it as theirs. If my song is exactly about your life right now, then it is. I don't even want to say that it's mine, because it's yours."

· • •

"In the public eye, girls and women with strong perspectives are hated. If you're a girl with an opinion, people just hate you. There are still people who are afraid of successful women, and that's so lame."

"You can write a song about being in love with someone, but you don't have to be in love with anyone."

. . .

"I've always been a singer. I never really decided I was gonna be a singer. It just kind of – I just sing a lot."

. . .

"Getting recognized is insane. It just blows my mind. Like, someone who you don't know at all can just be like, 'Oh my God – are you Billie?"

"

I'm a really particular person. I want it my way."

– Billie Eilish

"What makes a song last is real content from a mind that is thinking a little bit harder about certain things. A lot of artists don't really think that hard."

. • •

"Lyrics are so important, but they're really underrated."

. • •

"Pretty much my whole life, I've been a performer and have loved singing and writing songs in my room for my own ears."

Billie Eilish
THE LYRIC QUIZ

Can you name which songs these lyrics are from?

1   "Call me calloused, call me cold;
    You're italic, I'm in bold."

2   "I'm only good at being bad."

3   "I've been walking through a
    world gone blind; Can't stop
    thinking of your diamond mind."

4 "I'm biting my nails; I'm too young to go to jail."

5 "What do you want from me? Why don't you run from me?"

6 "Cause I, I'm in love with my future; Can't wait to meet her."

7 "Gold teeth, my neck, my wrist is froze."

8 "Fool me once, fool me twice; Are you death or paradise?"

9 "I don't want love I can't afford; I just want you to love for free."

10 "And all of these clouds crying us back to life, but you're cold as a knife."

11 "Will you only feel bad when they find out?"

12 "Count my cards watch them fall; Blood on a marble wall."

13 "Look at you needing me, You know I'm not your friend without some greenery."

14 "Maybe I should think about a new career; Somewhere in Kauai where I can disappear."

ANSWERS

How many did you get right?!

1. Copycat.
2. Bad Guy.
3. Ocean Eyes.
4. Bellyache.
5. Bury a Friend.
6. my future.
7. Bad Guy (with Justin Bieber).
8. No Time to Die.
9. Bored.
10. Six Feet Under.
11. Your Power.
12. You Should See Me in a Crown.
13. All The Good Girls Go to Hell.
14. NDA.

Billie Eilish
THE QUIZ

Now it's time to test your new knowledge on Billie! You can find the answers on the following page.

1 What is Billie's full name?

2 When is Billie's birthday?

3 Billie used to be scared of singing in front of people. True or false?

4 Where did Billie go to school?

5 What TV show inspired Billie's first song?

6 How tall is Billie?

7 What were the first two songs that Billie and Finneas recorded together?

8 What was Billie's second official single release?

9 At which festival did Billie first perform at?

10 When was Billie's first EP released?

11 How many Grammy awards did Billie win in 2020?

12 Billie was the first person born in the 2000's to have a number one album. True or false?

13 When was Billie's second studio album released?

14 What is the name of the song Billie and Finneas wrote for the latest James Bond movie?

15 Why was their 2021 Oscar nomination retracted?

16 What syndrome does Billie have that makes her have tics?

17 What suburb of Los Angeles did Billie and her family grow up in?

18 What instruments can Billie play?

19 What is the name of Billie's 2021 documentary?

20 What does NDA stand for?

ANSWERS

How many did you get right?!

1. Billie Eilish Pirate Baird O'Connell.
2. December 18th.
3. True!
4. She was homeschooled.
5. The Walking Dead.
6. 5 feet 3 inches (1.61 m).
7. She's Broken and Fingers Crossed.
8. Six Feet Under.
9. South by Southwest.
10. August 11, 2017.
11. Five.
12. True.
13. July 30th, 2021.
14. No Time to Die.
15. Because the movie release was delayed due to COVID-19.
16. Torrette's Syndrome.
17. Highland Park.
18. Piano, guitar and ukulele.
19. Billie Eilish: The World's a Little Blurry
20. Non-disclosure agreement.

Billie Eilish
WORD SEARCH

```
A L C M B B O R E D C X
Y G O U T R I V C X Z S
T R Y S Q U G L V C X O
R A U I A E S D L V Z U
S M G C J N G F D I U N
D M F I U D G V C X E D
M Y F U T U R E Q G R C
V S V J H F S A L C D L
C Z C N H G D E D E B O
X F I N N E A S C Z S U
Z L U G D E F G H B V D
C B O C E A N E Y E S C
```

Can you find all the words below in the wordsearch puzzle on the left?

BILLIE   MY FUTURE   GRAMMYS

FINNEAS   LOS ANGELES   BORED

SOUNDCLOUD   OCEAN EYES   MUSIC

Billie Eilish
CROSSWORD PUZZLE

Answer the clues and fill in the puzzle —good luck!

ACROSS

2. Grammy-winning Record of the Year in 2020
3. Movie she wrote a song for in 2023
5. Her clothing brand
7. Her starsign
8. Her brother
11. Her surname
12.   First single

DOWN

1. Popstar she's loved since a child
4. Her diet
6. Hometown
9. Song with Khalid
10. Her family dog's name

Solutions

	L		M		B	O	R	E	D		
	G	O	U			I					S
	R		S			L					O
	A		I	A			L				U
	M		C	N				I			N
	M				G				E		D
M	Y	F	U	T	U	R	E				C
	S						L				L
								E		O
	F	I	N	N	E	A	S			S	U
										D
	O	C	E	A	N	E	Y	E	S	

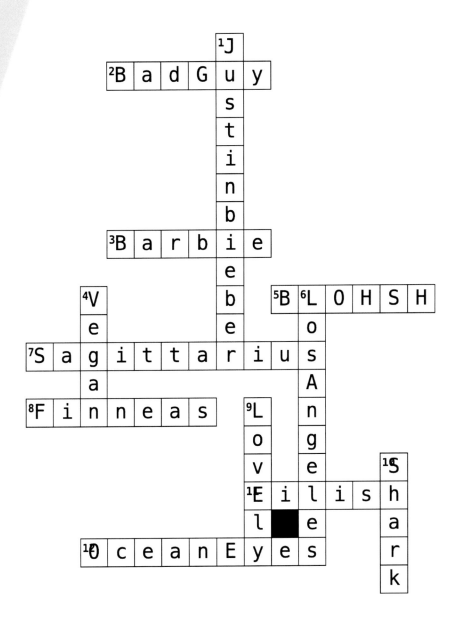

We hope you learnt some
awesome facts about
Billie!

What was your
favourite? How did you do in
the quiz? Let us know in a
review—we'd love to hear
from you!

For more great books,
visit us at
www.bellanovabooks.com.

Milton Keynes UK
Ingram Content Group UK Ltd.
UKRC030300020424
440455UK00005B/62